SHERANNE SHEA JUBELIRER
& JEFFREY DAVID JUBELIRER

How We Said

PRAYERS

and BELIEVE

GOD

ALMIGHTY

Heard Us

Faith And Graces

Quantum
Discovery
A LITERARY AGENCY

ISBN
978-1-963254-30-3 (Paperback)
978-1-963254-31-0 (eBook)

HOW WE SAID PRAYERS AND BELIEVE GOD ALMIGHTY HEARD US

TABLE OF CONTENTS

PICKING UP MY CROSS OF CHRIST JESUS

Issues of life out of the Truth to perceive
righteous inquiries
that may lead to mystical revelations
that I have seen as I am a lay catholic mystic and
visionary.
Of laying down the ego
to deny flesh
to pick up Jesus on the Cross
and to walk with God Almighty
with joy
and hopefulness
by overcoming in moments of weakness
while we live upon overshadowing experiences of graces
and that anointing of the Holy Spirit
as God reigns forever more
by that's the truth given.

By SherAnne Shea Jubelirer

OPEN DOOR REVERIE

Prayerfully, very prayerfully to experience
More of enlightenment by expanding my mind of open
reverie
With wonders I do imagine possibilities
Particularly of mystical things
With the eeking out the door of images
Making an etch by light streaming
With thoughts of royal spiritedness.
And you can see that's my interesting face beaming
With an artist's smile
Contemplating the dusk reaching out
Whenever even was come
For that's only my father somewhere further in the
rosy glory
To make you feel more open
To my imaginations and for holy purity
While I do seek a good place for expression and writings
Within growing visions of ethereal hopefully
spiritual creatures
Like famous saints or faithful holy angels standing near
the fire
As we call
With that's of my father's days as hero,
With running free
To the other side of heaven.
God is there!

By SherAnne Shea Jubelirer

OF THIS SACRIFICE
WAS JESUS, HIMSELF

Sacrifice of Jesus's love,
A spiritual reality in heaven and on earth.
Obedience is more acceptable than His sacrifice was true.
Pure truth molded into form
Out of goodness then comes willingness to be faithful.
For some, not counting the cost
Nor looking outward
instead looking within to find God's desires of
holy truths
Shaping each soul.

By SherAnne Shea Jubelirer

THAT'S LOVE POETRY FOR JEFF AND SHERANNE

Look I want to share every experience
I ever had with you.
We trust one another
And we are unique people
Who must discover our own identities together to pull
each other out of the fire back
Towards our professional and personal developments
through faith
And that's love.
So I do only wish for you to be strong in Jesus for us
Then whenever I do need you
I will find comfort in our strength and that's wisdom.

By SherAnne Shea Jubelirer

ON THAT'S DAILY
ROUTINES FOR NOW

And again who I was again doing my morning pages.
For I was watching Christian, catholic programming.

And I do try to create a spiritual awakening everyday.
We do have that holy day and that work day. And now
I am coming to Saint William's today. I do come often
to Saint William's True, Holy Roman Catholic Church.
I do think Saint William's was and has been onward for
all of us, for that's mine every where else and they were
prayed for everyday. Or we are nevers, all of us Shea's, us
Keifers and us Shea Jubelirer's.

Alright now, I was back from Saint William's. I did
prayers and we were doing prayers for everyone.

For the whole church was for all of us on this holy day.
And I do that. My mother said everyday is a holy day.
We were praying over the dew fall in the liturgy. For
a place of refreshment. Light and peace for those who
have already died in my family.

I will hopefully do some facial masks as that's a beauty
secret. I was treating myself for working hard so I
bought 3 real good masks on QVC. And I do love
truths and beauty and fashion. So I must begin to
organize and clean up and use beauty products in my
containers.

And we do pray for those in the hospitals: for healing, for deliverance, for life, for understanding, for love, for peace, for wisdom.

By SherAnne Shea Jubelirer

LOVE POETRY

On living completely all alone with God
And living all on my own
Yet I am in love with him.
He is often doing things by himself.
I do await him each day for I do hope to win
The poet's affection and love.
He loves to talk continuously
And respond and listen I would,
For his excitement strengthens myself.
His passion and desire I must win.
For golden could our life become and new Catholic
beginnings
And new days
Together we would be experiencing
And happiness is very important!

By SherAnne Shea Jubelirer

MAYBE THIS IS REALITY FOR NOW

And this piece of writing is on to do. How I look on for now. Except this is reality, that we need on for everything. How any writings and any of that's our books were on and on and on.

I do remember I over heard an old lady and she wanted something on.

I am supposed to be more an on, only then I have been. We have been here for over 30 years. Maybe very little is on here. Author does take very little right here. And I am to do, that's clear. And I do like to do this and I do like to do that, as Lettie had given me this right here.

I only slept 5 hours, which is good.

And now there is music that we are playing. I am listening to R & B classics, Donna Summer, Quincy Jones

And the like.

Michael Jackson was on music choice tonight and I thought own him. My own to do that. And so that's that!

Now I am listening to Van Morrison singing into the mystic. I am a lay catholic mystic and visionary. My mother told me, I was mystic. And she was right whenever she told me that.

I can write anymore for this topic of mysticism. Hopefully I will do so.

TO LIVE HERE IN PHILLY

Of people right around Only Us Authors,
I am supposed to ignore
And be doing prayers to do so right here..
And we are attending Saint William's
And that helps us tremendously.
That's my holy day of obligation was already met.
We do come to Saint William's every chance we can to
be in Saint William's.
And now I can take this gorgeous Saint Joseph,
pray for us!
For we are devoted to labor
And good works
And I do devotions,
That I do like to do daily and consistently
And you, holy Saint Joseph are supposed to protect us.
And likewise thee Blessed Virgin Mary is protection
And graces for us…

By SherAnne Shea Jubelirer

THAT'S ANOTHER GIFT FROM GOD ALMIGHTY

The simplicity of light,
Brilliant in truth
Dispelling darkness
Giving sight
Precious element
Of fire and sun
Electrically that's fixed to radiate on
And on
Pragmatically granted
Forever needed
Of glory found presence with beauty
And strength to guide.

By SherAnne Shea Jubelirer

WE ARE SO FAR AND WHOLESOMELY AND EVERYWHERE AND GONE

We have come so far
And God does maintain us
And He cares
And He will forever love us Shea's, us Keifer's...
Absolutely God will take care of us!
Even if we do die,
We will live in heaven
And God Almighty is forever faithful and true.
That's of the promises of God and Christ.
We must only believe and love Him
And choose to obey Him.
We must keep ourselves optimistic
And of that's true
And of honesty
And of truthfulness
And of good integrity.
We must choose to grow
And develop of that our most holy faith
And look for graces to be added
Whenever we do prayers and devotions
And receive of the sacramentals in holy, true
catholic churches.
God is constantly pouring out His Blessings on us.
And kindness
And gentleness
And forgiveness are required.

By SherAnne Shea Jubelirer

TODAY I SAW

Shimmering rays of sunlight
Bouncing and splashing
And reflected through tree lined bohemian, hippie
street.
Lined by art, glamour, promises and time.
Get a way, go have a good day
Turn South in the city
To be glancing and seeing paintings in picture windows
made up
Of pretty, unusual
Sometimes bizarre things.

South Street
Do it up, make a day, buy a book,
Sip, sip, sip on coffee and cream
Get into the scene!

ON THE BEACH IN JUNE

White capped ocean waves flow forth like our
conversation
As that's only my father and that's only me were walking
the five miles out
On the dusky beach, very near the home my father owns.
We do take that's only home has been absolutely
everywhere.
We were talking of God Almighty, how we were with
others, the obstacles put in the Way
And my future.
We will overcome because we do mean a great deal to
God Almighty.
I do realize the power of living a good life, full of self
control and gratitude.
I do think of all my father's spirituality will become
And times my mother had spoken of his closeness
to God.
That's inspiration was given to him by the Lord Jesus.
But what is important on this day in June was whatever
the future promises in our search of truths And who
God Almighty is.
What is important is that we learn from our experiences
So that we may grow holy
For the rest of our days
While we are here upon this earth
And how we hope God Almighty can make our souls
into complete holiness
By our gifts of faith in Jesus and Mary
As we live each and everyday in graces.

OF BEST OF BELIEVING WHENEVER I CAN

O my Jesus, help me! I am called and chosen to be a saint as all are.

Also the Truth, that I felt and sensed that anointing of the Holy Spirit on

Several occasions whenever I was reading the Holy Scriptures, doing prayers

And meditating and doing contemplations on certain scriptures. Mostly with Jesus,

This is by faith, that's by faith, that gift of faith that I do possess where I can receive

Jesus thru Mary.

And I do have a few certain people I can trust and believe like my mother and my father

And priests and doctors and Jeff.

April 2010
By SherAnne Shea Jubelirer

WITH CHRIST JESUS

With Christ Jesus always able to abound with all
graces for
That's sufficiency to me all ways with all things
As I do purpose in my heart
For each and every good work
I do with each and every good writing that I do for
I do have joy to think of these writings and that this
very day.

Relaxing and doing my writings right here on Saturday,
September 12, 2009

With only Truth, that little pretty pup by me.
Comfortable and that song "Hello Dolly"

Is playing on the big band and music station.

This way up here is my very good writing career since I
get so little feedback and yet

That's pleasing to me whenever I get a book published.
However and whenever I will be getting more exposure
for my books, maybe some money will be made. And
maybe I will make some money with my good works,
every good poem and each line of poetry. And likewise
writing creative non-fiction and spiritual memoirs.

I was at a restaurant and reading that's my first book, a
few poems didn't seem like that much to me

Except only then whenever I was home by myself, the poetry that I had written was perfectly fine.

I do strive for both consistency and constancy especially with my writings. Ah, the life of an Author Only,

Writer and Poet always shows me new things to think of and write of. Life does carry on for me as I am truly honey and I do love to bother no one.

Without were fightings, within was fear.

O my sweet Holy Jesus, I do truly believe in your love for me.Help me to keep on growing and experiencing personal and professional development. My doing readings and learning teachings truly can be that's necessary. O this loneliness won't seem to do me the Way I do desire to be finished.

O heck, I do suppose this writing is only alright. Maybe I do need to take some more good actions. Later.

The pope, Benedict XVI said, "that faith is the spirit of intelligence." Praise Jesus! I do find coming along to church today was brilliant for me. For we can be singing in church and with a lady named Mary, we will be singing! And receiving Christ Jesus in holy communion, where the Blessed Sacrament will greatly inspire someone like me.

September 14, 2009
By SherAnne Shea Jubelirer

LOOK FOR NOW

Look for now, I sure do realize all these words and any books with good ideas

That this Author Only has its written and was published for treasured readers and book buyers,

For that does make me know and wonder how far is my reach through my books now? I will write this line telling you this book will have been in far and gone places with God Almighty in every place,

That I have reached bringing or making for you my imaginations and memories as I took to think over here and will write on anything that's given by that faith, that hope and that love sown on in God Almighty that I do have of that anointing of life in the Holy Spirit.

Where as this was sown in the Catholic Churches, where we do belong or watch on Eternal Word Network and that's of prayers, we made to Jesus and have won for our salvation and of that's love and that's eternal life that we receive often of Jesus, the Christ. We have been realizing that God loves us and cares for us so maybe now, we can receive God's rest and remember things have been over to do for now. And right now, our books and things have been doing real fine.

Tomorrow will come with renewed hope and new ideas to tell us so. Or to do has been of that's mine, for God is so good and we will only believe and keep right on working.

August 16, 2022
By SherAnne Shea Jubelirer

OCTOBER 30, 2010

Holiness!
Holy were the prayers
That were all said.
Holy were the praises
That were all made to the Lord Jesus on high.
Holy were the dreams
That we were seeing...
Holy were our thoughts upon paper.
Holy was that day
When the dancer and I were talking of and reading
about holy angels,
Holy were the angels, I have somehow seen.
Holy was my love for you
While before in holiness and righteousness.
Holy, holy, holy was and is Jesus, the God of
all creation,
Holy is eternity!

ON THIS IS HOWEVER I HAVE BEEN FOR ANY WHERE, RIGHT NOW

I did make to do that everyday for a while...everyday is a holy day, that's my mother told me so.

And so that holy day and that work day is done everyday to the Lord Jesus Christ.

And already I said my morning prayers from the Divine Office For Hours. And good sound sleep, for I slept and slept for hours and hours and right now I am refreshed and rejuvenated. And on holidays, I was feeling the Very Same Way with my folks over in New Jersey, wholesomely at the shore for that's again.

At Saint William's Holy, True Catholic Church, I was invited to do the very same. And to do the very same like Jesus is very good for us. O how I long to do the same as whenever I was working, I would work before writing books. And I am a book writer and I can take a gorgeous look on that's my past and that's beautiful of me. And for beauty and brains and money, often I have been.

And of these great United States Of America, I have been to do that everywhere. Except myself as that's only one of us here. I am somewhere often and wholesomely.

O how I want to be yours, Jesus and yours I only wish to be and as Jesus's I only wish to do that.

Whenever Jesus, will you come for me?

And of beauty sleep, I was able to get so much! Thank you so very much, Holy Spirit!

June 26, 2016
By SherAnne Shea Jubelirer

HOW EVERYTHING HAS BEEN DOING ALRIGHT

Seeking to give thanks to God Almighty for this is the right Way to give thanks to Him for this is the Day the Lord has made so let us make and do our prayers and give thanks to God, the Divine Mercy of which is holy marriage where the messanic jewish poet looks dapper and I was fuller in Christ Jesus and will be fulfilled. For mercy, our hope of God's mercy by that the Sacred Heart of Jesus of this poster, picture that we gaze on and meditate on will help us in prayers and of that's love so we will be satisfied and pleased to anticipate whatsoever God has in store for us and whenever we are doing devotions and prayers in church. For now, we make everything has been doing alright. Let us reach for heaven!

By SherAnne Shea Jubelirer

THAT'S OF THE LIGHT DAWNING

And this is a great, new day of awakening
Upon the dawn
Of prayerful beginnings of new days.
We are able
Now of opportunities
For friendship and good works
Willed by God
With sanctity of moments in prayers
And that's newness to behold by our hearts of golden,
reverencing graces
For the Only, True God
Of the holy hours,
Who forever keeps our souls and spirits
To grow by illuminations of truths learned.

By SherAnne Shea Jubelirer

ON SHERRY'S RELATIONSHIPS

But the neighborhood is very problematic. They are divorced, too sexual, they cause trouble.But they are just mere people. There is over people. I was experiencing difficulty so I said under them 9's. And now I am taking the 25 and the 25 since I do got Kelly's boys. And that's true, that's all of my whole family, well they were all 9's. I have been doing as that's a 10 for now. Whenever we do get to church, we do that's 7's. They all should be that's 7's since money is so tight and hard to earn for these days. Like I said, I do got all kinds of family and several friends. And they were as good as they were mine. And that's only mine and for now this is mine. Blessed assurance , Jesus the Christ is that's mine.

I am God Almighty's child and as far as my siblings children, they are children of God. We are very good professionals, and now we do have 7 MBA's and Kelly's boys would like to become MBA's so we will be of 9 MBA's and 2 Authors Only, Writers and Poets and we do have 3 RN's and that's my father's doing for he was a very successful CEO and President and he was the Chairman of the Board at Cape May Regional Hospital. My beautiful mother was just only a very good housekeeper. For that's my whole family is very well educated and does work professionally. My family does or that's done deals or that's assignments or we even do that's powers of agreements. We will grow in wisdom and holiness, God willing! I do pray often that we will be holy and happy and healthy.

By SherAnne Shea Jubelirer

OF GOD ALMIGHTY,
I DO SEE SIGNS AND WONDERS

Such wonders upon dreams of great writings and launching our writing careers in 2010. Us 2 poets and writers and Authors Only profoundly in love and living the writing life and holy life together. Our dreams of seeing miraculous brilliant thoughts of things that we are thinking will be very well put together upon the written pages and in that's our books. Both of us do have such holy dreams with hope arising. Truly for that now, truly only then. We can begin to see great things happening in our connections and works. Joy is evident. We will work on ever to grow on these holy dreams and sought after visions where freedom and rights of priviledge are actualized and the life of Jesus inside of souls and spirits are truly that's maintained until we become ashes and dust. Till we are with Jesus.

SUMMER 1981

Look I have been out to San Francisco, California, all of Summer 1981. I was on a school program, HECUA, Higher Education Consortitum Urban Academics Affairs.

When I was at the University Of San Francisco, I was working as a probation aid at South Of Market Intake, a youth dention facility for juvenile delinguents. I was only 21 years old myself so my sense of authority with kids who stole a car and they were joyriding. Well, I was never tough enough.

I was taking 2 classes with this program as well. I do remember working with another probation aid.

I thought he was very good at work. I do remember when he told me, na. I remember a child had a gun

And that caused a death to happen. And I do remember they picked up a young girl doing street walking

And she had absolutely no business doing it. She was walking the street in Oakland, California. I earned all B's in the program. Mostly for work, I was writing disposition reports at South Of Market Intake out in San Francisco.

Randy Wong was working at South Of Market Intake. He decided to show San Francisco to me. We studied Haight-Ashbury neighborhood of old Victorian houses and Haight-Ashbury had a shopping community district with diners and stores and the hippies walking past. I do remember the hippies saw me and said, "There, she is!" We were talking.

The summer of love was in 1969 in that area. The 1960's in San Francisco was crazy love and wild.

The beat poets in the 1960's were from that area.

Whenever I was at University of San Francisco, I got to be doing lunch with the nun who had taught the class that I took called UNDERTANDING THE NEW TESTAMENT at Saint John's University. I do remember, she told me to be quiet. And I do remember I was happy to see her.

At the front desk, I met a very good friend where that friendship and romance took place

In San Francisco, New York City and New Jersey. His name was Vahan Backman Goursidan. We had a romantic and very nice relationship. We were good friends but he disappeared. He was rich and mulatto.

JANUARY 26, 1995

The year we came to Narcotics Anonymous,
The year we began calling LeSea Prayerline.

I am angry right now. My folks say they want to fix up
my house and then sell it. Suppose they do, I won't have
it. For I do like living inside of here.

I am quoting the holy scriptures and praying about
receiving healing. I truly wish I was more mystical.
Seeing Christ in the holy scriptures is about finding the
ultimate reality of life. All the answers are right in the
Word Of God. It was inspiring and awesome when I
was reading the testimony of the Lord Jesus Christ is
the Spirit of prophesy. I do believe I do have the gift of
faith. I must make the effort to feed my mind on the
Word Of God.

By SherAnne Shea Jubelirer

GLADNESS AND HAPPINESS

2022

Gladness and happiness is happening having been able to come across 40 notebooks of that's mine.

That all was written and that through a long while now.

They were written by ourselves carefully and truthfully and rightfully with hope

That we put together upon paper in notebooks to build together our very good writing careers,

By the Poet since 1968 whenever Jeffrey David Jubelirer began writing and I, another poet and writer since 1985.

Hard work and strong effort are required for us to make progress and achieve and accomplish so very much.

We both do write consistently and often and we are always looking for things to write as we do the necessary things with our writing life even if regular life requires of us to take care of ourselves with other areas of life like doing daily living skills. That must do for we have learned that God daily loadeth us with benefits and we seek to follow Jesus, the Christ and stay focused wherever we maybe on writing projects. We yearn to be stars with writings and any books and likewise also seek to live the holy life through the Catholic Churches and prayers consistently and readings of holy books and the bible and we do reach out to the prayerlines.

We are real fine poets and writers, us Authors Only and personally my forte' is spirituality and Catholicism and mysticism and theology and doing writings.

Maybe some day we will do more interviews while reading our finished works and books and perhaps this will be for posterity and to educate our treasured readers.

November 24, 2008
By SherAnne Shea Jubelirer

ON MY THOUGHTS AND OF WRITINGS HERE

Puzzled by lack of payment for many, many pieces of writing and publications and any books.

As I am only genius as only an Author, Writer and Poet. Its poetic and literary and creative and catholic of me. I am desiring greater credentials and accolades.

For years, I had to do anything for the art of it and that's great except for future days, more money is required. And my need of more godly friends is likewise another desire. I so want to experience maybe assessing my needs and making some plans are what I must do. I do realize I am supposed to be happy

And share my life with someone. And the love of my life has left me again. And interests I do need to keep on developing and experiencing. Maybe to do some more writings that require research is necessary. And of book ideas, I do have a few.

And as far as men, I get offers everyday whenever I take walks. And yet I am here with God alone.

What are my priorities and for prior things of truth and beauty, that has left me wondering?

Nor does the power of God and wisdom of God come so easily whenever I have been receiving Christ Jesus some, many years as 30 years at Saint William's True,

Holy, Roman Catholic Church. And practicing the presence of God is acquired by so much pursuit of Him.

And I am a lay catholic mystic and visionary that comes from that seeking of God regularly of visions and of dreams, God does give me. And I do realize I do possess Him for real and that's so true.

And while I do know God is ever faithful and true. And I can depend on that.

Of nocturia is all kinds of dreams that come to me at night since I take 200 milligrams of seroquel that makes me dream often.

Its interesting and of real dreams and spiritual awakenings.

Hope for some more love and truths fulfill my heart and mind here,,,

---

December 19, 2016
By SherAnne Shea Jubelirer

ON LIVING @HASBROOK

On Living @Hasbrook, That's Only SherAnne's Living
Legacy and That's Only Jeff's Living Legacy

Tired of trying so hard here, I find depression in my
beautiful soul and everyone says I am so beautiful
indeed. I hope that lasts and like I am last to do right
here. Concern of becoming older and I do seek to do the
Will Of God everyday and Jeffrey has to be taking care
of business right here. And that's as my true will, exactly
to do like Jesus, the Christ.

For maybe and yes, that's good sound sleep and dreams
that will refresh and beautify myself and I will make
a few prayers for family and loves everyday to ease my
mind that's together on that of God Almighty.

And that's love for my beloved is real and Fixer likewise
and I do try to be true for him. I was given by some
kind neighbors, Doris and Rick, that I do that's always
true for Jeff.

I am trusting God Almighty and I will keep that's on.

By SherAnne Shea Jubelirer

FOR NOW

For now, I am living by myself for Holy God.
Hopefully my folks can keep on living for God as
very well.
They truly bless me and give me anything that I desire
or may need.
They have been extremely good to me and I sure picked
the right folks For that will all of my life be fulfilled.
Which is ever lasting life likewise.
I truly do need a new soulmate because the poet left me
because he was Fighting. I had all of that forgiven by the
priest And according to the bible.
Thank God for the gift of life
And gifts of wisdom and understanding.
For true knowledge is the Way to wisdom
And life. These writings are and were only pieces that
hopefully I will Keep working with.
I will have readers especially whenever we get
marketing programs
For our books.
They were beautiful, brilliant, holy books.
And its written as truthfully
And honestly I can put forth these powerful words
on paper
And or as ebooks, paper backs and hard backs.
I love to do as a real pretty writer and poet.
That's my style and the Way to do that for I am then.
God is so good
And the Lord does provide.
Hope ought to reign

And all of us must sow great peace, us Shea's, us Keifer's
With our lives and loves.
Whenever I did look for what was now around I saw
how they were very gone
And living other places. Hopefully they work hard and
love one another.

HOLY LIFE IN DAYS, WEEKS AND HOURS

And some days. Life is so hard living over in my old
house.
Whatsoever was so good is hard now.
We are only Authors together.
God Almighty is our best life
And the love of God is of the higher things
That we must learn to maintain
And keep on believing for.
That's all we need is love.
We do have our claim to fame
Since we both created and made evenly, for
That's all 26 books now.
Telling the priests
And asking how we will continue on is
That's a goal.
I will talk and confess to the priest
For this great afternoon,
That will help to console us
And feed our spirits and souls of that holy faith
And holy graces
Since we take Jesus, the Christ at His Word
And in holy communion.
God Almighty owns everything.
Let us keep on in prayers!

By SherAnne Shea Jubelirer

HERE WE LOOK AT TELEVISION

And seeing on certain programs about God.
We do believe
And love to be told
On all that new things that we do realize
And we do prayers often
Thrice or more everyday
And prayers give us focus
And make us productive.
Whenever we are done
And we must trust
And have faith in God that He Will and Does
answer prayers.
For us Authors Only do have answers
And questions
As we persevere
And keep right on praying
And choose to do well
And so we depend on God Almighty's Mercy,
forever more..

February 7, 2021
By SherAnne Shea Jubelirer

WHENEVER I WAS 50 YEARS OLD

For some years, I thought about writing a novel. I had begun a novel but never completed that book.

I was questioning how interesting such a book would be. Then whenever I was in a bookstore over in University City, I bought a book called "How To Write Your Own Autobiographical Novel."

Here I am living in Philadelphia where I was struggling as a Writer and Poet. I yearn to be brighter and brilliant. I have since then only learned that I am only genius as Only an Author. I do yearn to be more fulfilled of life but I do find my life is difficult at best. The mistakes I made along the Way have caused me suffering. Smoking is suffering. Now here today I am on my 12th day of no cigarettes. I do try not to bother people living in this neighborhood. I do not bother! I never can tell because over here they were bothering.

I am only learning that my thought life is more of reality and self existent and real to me for I make up or determine a great deal of how I do respond with whatever happens to me by the things I am thinking of right here...What makes life difficult for me is the subjectivity that we all experience and everyone is different.

At a time, like this, I do feel that regular facts and the Truth, Jesus, HimSelf can make life dealing with manic depression, an easier task. Medicine helps correct this disease. I am an overcomer and I do believe I am very cleared up and healed by a great deal of prayers and Jesus. Sure, its terrible to suffer with voices from the medicine and over this insomnia and I had some nervousness and depression.

I do now suffer just only over this insomnia. And medicine works! I do find the Way shows that's possible or even probable to cope. To live in harmony with disease. However, over the years 1 have been in denial.

Very deep denial. I do try to make myself as good of a soul and spirit. I did join the Carmelites in 2000 and was with this program until 2002. By prayers, 3 times a day structured by the Divine Office Of the Catholic Church, I have chosen to make spirituality and Jesus along with the saints to do for my way of coping. I do often think of the holy angels as well. I do say and think or the holy angels whenever I do find that's necessary here. I was taught the Way of Perfection by the Carmelite program and so I do seek perfection and perfect moments.

Now however my life is of being a real attractive and pretty 50 year old and I am a writer and poet and as an Author Only is now difficult at best because of health concerns. Maybe I was worrying and however I do realize I do have the gift of faith and trust and believe that God will take care of all of us and its for whenever I grow older that I will have so very much work and writings to have shown for that. The bible says I will yet live God's Way and I do chose to walk in His Ways as best I can do that. I do have hope for our days! Today is the day the Lord has made so we will rejoice and be glad. I do keep looking up to Jesus and imagining Him with me. I do try to count on the Lord more than ever. "To will, the Will Of God everyday! I am someone who does the Will Of God everyday. For these were the things of Jesus that I truly do. The Will of God is Jesus and Jesus has healing and full deliverance of all that I am doing in thoughts and has brought that's necessary for my mind. All is well.

What I had fear of was the future state of my health. I do feel like I would be a potential train wreck, honestly. Since I was living alone for a while, God is the Only One that I could trust for this day.

THAT'S MORE FOR FAMILY AND FRIENDS AND HOW WE ARE NEVERS, FOR THAT'S FAR AND GONE

For now everyday is a great, new day to begin with. Today I was listening to my records and tapes. And music covers over my slight negativity about the neighbors. They can be nasty and terrible sometime.

They never give us anymore. Next door, it was a prostitute that stole a lot of stuff out of our holy house.

So we said they are not needed. I am trying to be supportive and loyal to Robert and Steve Gaynor and absolutely Jeff. And now I do have 9 girlfriends, counting my two cousins, Shawn and Deb. I do got Helene, Gena, Sylvania and Eileen and Dorothy. Kelly, my sister never calls us, maybe she calls monthly. I was looking for paid work. Jeff gave me 2 manuscripts to type up for $100.oo per manuscript.

This journaling is to help me get writing again. And likewise, to help restore my creativity and restore my creative energies. I sure do like experimenting and playing with my pens and notebooks.

For I would like to create a dream and gratitude journal.
My gratitude is deep for my mother and father and Jeff.
They have given us that's everything and that's done
of everything else far and gone and for that's right here
in America.

My father and mother re-filled up out of our house of all
that was stolen over 2015.

March 25, 2021
By SherAnne Shea Jubelirer

ETERNALLY, THAT'S NECESSARY LOVE THROUGH THE TRUTH

Experiences bring about days of time
For great hope
Through gates of prayers
Giving me that's purpose
And I do realize that's my God given purpose to make
beautiful, brilliant, holy books.
To open a growing knowledge and love of truths
Manifesting that's eternal life in the souls,
I do only see by the Holy Spirit…
For who can bring all to that's love by the truth
And thee Truth is this is the Christ Jesus before all.
And suffering and hope are promised in the Holy
Scriptures…

By SherAnne Shea Jubelirer

ETERNAL JOY!

Praise be to the Lord Jesus Christ
And of this was glory to God
And of my that's of my father, he was my glory
And he said that's my books were my love and glory!
Even in my agony and emotional pain
I will rejoice!
For even if my beloved leaves me again
I shall joy in my Savior!
Jesus reigneth.
With hope I will cry to my King.
I shall take joy!

By SherAnne Shea Jubelirer

DAYS AND NIGHTS AND SLEEP!

Drifts into sleep, good sound sleep
And dreams is of great interest
And that's necessary for us
As I do make and do prayers in the night watches.
And I do realize that's dreams that come by God's
Holy Love to us.
And together on the bed,
We do like to think of days
And life
And cuddle with Fixer,
A very good little dog
That we both love so much here.
Truthfully I did so very much more right here..

By SherAnne Shea Jubelirer

MUCH NEEDED PRAYERS

I am doing prayers the Lord Jesus will sanctify and bless me for this life now. That's enough for me to become a very well educated writer and poet. Its the desire of my heart to do that's all kinds of writings.

I do think I can study religion and read all the holy books and hopefully I can do writings and maybe teaching on the side. I would never question God's intelligence so why must I question my abilities and talents? God willing, I will be blest.

Somebody prayed for me and he said I would find much favor with God and man.

A LOVE AFFAIR WITH JEFF

At the beginning of today,
I do think I am supposed to pray.
Everyone around me is so quiet.
I live in the joy of the Lord for its strength.
I was thinking of having you,
You who say things to me
So I hear things.
You must remember but no one will say how you do.
Some may say why I do but I am only the writer of this
chickee few words here…
Thank you very much!

By SherAnne Shea Jubelirer

THAT'S BEAUTIFUL OF HOW WE DO PRAYERS AND HOLY DEVOTIONS EVERYDAY

And this is the acceptable year of the Lord and Savior,
Jesus Christ
And that's often said by us here. And this is every year up
till now.
And wherever we begin to wonder and think of God's signs and
wonders
And we do remember where we have been in that's past days
For we will look back and true stories of us come again
And memories and remembrances that we have experienced
make us all realize
We have come too far so we do remember this and that.
We do have a map of the United States on my library-study wall.
And that's how I will write this book. To point and remember
And write,
And to write and to remember
Where I have been and we have been
Using honesty and truthfulness
And of very good integrity, in order to write books
And I do write of and on anything that's fine that I can think of
That I will like to write and create like I do already have 9 books
where its written
And completed and was published.
And that's book #10 right here! For this book is called
Before We Said Prayers And God Has Heard Us In Word
And Deed.
Heaven Sent!

Note to Saint Williams

And so to write of experiences of coming to her Saint William's True Holy Roman Catholic Church is almost always a very good experience. And I do believe that's good stuff does happen and good things do happen together whenever we are in the church. Together we are doing prayers and we receive Christ Jesus in holy communion frequently. And we do like coming to church during weekdays, come high noon day. We all pray together and sing a holy sacrament song at holy communion and some days, we do pray the Holy Rosary and we say a few words to each other after Mass.

Saint William's has events and dinners occasionally. We had been to the 100th Centennial dinner and dance gathering. We had so much fun that holy evening. 3 ladies were on the dance floor and they motioned me to dance and so we danced to some great music. That was a great experience.

Whenever we are in Saint William's, we read of the Holy Scriptures together. Recently we were in the Book Of Acts and the Gospel Of Saint Luke.. I do believe in the catholic church and I have been to many catholic churches in Philly and else where for I have been to Saint Rita's, Saint John Neumann's Shrine and Saint Patrick's and Miraculous Medal Shrine and Saint Jude Holy Church in Monroe, Ct.

Likewise, I have been to Saint Peter and Saint Paul Holy Baslica And Saint Paul's in Stone Harbor, New Jersey and Maria Stella, Saint Brendon, the Navigator in

Avalon, New Jersey; and that was of others such as we do prayers for everyone and I do pray that for the nuns and priests. We now are taught and given preparations by 3 holy, sweet, wonderful priests at Saint William's, Fr. Eugene is likewise a priest at Saint William's. Fr. Al, Fr. Gus and Fr. Tariq Issac. They have been teaching and preaching catholic , Christian social teachings to us. He is one true God forever and ever!

When I was at Saint John's University, I took a class taught by a priest called CHRISTIAN, SOCIAL TEACHINGS. I received a B for that class.

We were raised in the Catholic Churches. We did belong to Mary, Mother Of The Church, in Burnsville, Minnesota. My father was that lectern and my brothers were altar boys. They were newspaper boys as well.

AS WE LOOK TO CREATE A SPIRITUAL AWAKENING DAILY

And of a certain flow,
Yet God has the overflow of words and prayers
And books on my library book cases.
As we do reach family and friends on the phone.
We do watch Eternal Word Network
And God does make an eternal offering for us
And salvation is received
And acquired through prayers made daily.
We have a new beginning everyday
Whenever we wake up and believe.
And again and again
We do pray that
And spiritually believe and receive
Jesus, the Christ.

The Litany of Thee Blessed Virgin Mary was on today
And so to do that of intercessions is that's a good idea
And I did already do prayers for everyone
And I was given to do prayers for all of us
And so I do prayers for that everyday.
And now I am supposed to call my sweet, wonderful
Holy father, Richard Authur Shea in the morning.
They were always together,
That's only my mother's doing and that's only my
father's doing, They were always together.
God is so good
And we do have to do good
And choose to be good for one another,
That's what we said together.

By SherAnne Shea Jubelirer

EASTER SUNDAY 2021

And again doing for my morning pages. For I was
watching Christian, catholic programming. That's a
wonderful way to begin each day for God's mercies
are that's new every morning. And I do try to create
a spiritual awakening everyday. And we do create and
make that holy day and that work day. Everyday is a
great, new day to begin with.

Alright now, to begin again writing this book right here.
So I have been before in over 31 states of America. And
for only these days, I do take walks like today. I was
walking almost over 38 minutes. 20 minutes to Saint
William's And back, this over 18 minutes to Spanish
store and coming back. And walking out on the street
of NorthEast Philly area. They say for a whole people so
that gives me that's true freedom, American style. For
this happy Easter Sunday. We were already in church.
We were listening to the Holy Scriptures. And we were
singing in church. Fr. Al gave a great sermon. And after
Mass, he gave us a beautiful postcard of Saint William's
that says GRATEFUL AND BLESSED.

I truly do love and believe the prayers of the
Holy Liturgy.

A NOTE TO JESUS, THE CHRIST

Precious Savior that hope of your mercy, my sweet
holy Jesus, I do come to stand by You and I have won
salvation and anymore prayers, to do that all again, God
willing, I will do. I do write this to you now.
Please, Jesus make my life full by prayers, by church,
by doing readings and by doing writings and by that's
love, by family and always by my soul mate who can
welcome me to live and grow with him. Lord Jesus
Christ, I do say thank you so very much! May You, Jesus
forevermore reign and rule us.

Sunday April 26, 2009
By SherAnne Shea Jubelirer

2010

People who were coming to church…

Who were making great prayers,

Who were the religious and the laity

Who looked up to the religious

And aspired to be like such ones.

Who were dancing as a stripper in fancy places.

TO WORK AND HAVING THAT WORKS WITH THE PRIESTS AND THE CHURCH

And the Truth is Jesus, the Christ Himself. And real truths are a real dynamic between the priest and myself. My trouble is I think that I am in love with him. However, that would never happen and our priest is so holy, that's probably just a phase I am experiencing. We love him so very much. I like him too much.

Maybe its that I truly like him. I do remember I told my mother and she had said "forget it!"

Its now no problem and and maybe it's a real joy to work with the priests.

By SherAnne Shea Jubelirer

ON PRAISE, ON LOVE AND ON WORSHIP OF JESUS, THE CHRIST WITH THEE BLESSED MOTHER, MARY MOST HOLY

For making that of peace
And that's of goodness
And prayers
And we do choose to do of that everyday
For we do have that work day and that holy day,
Now and forever.
God Almighty is of 7 Spirits.
He is Divine Spirit of spirits.
We have given Him, our life together.
And He does give us real life back
And good sound sleep and dreams.
God does love us and cares for us.
We sure do believe for all of these of us Shea's
And us Keifers for God Almighty like we sure were,
We sure have been or of nevers together
And Jesus is so powerful, we are made well and
wholesome by Him
And for that's love since that's all we need is love.
May God Almighty and Jesus and of the Holy Spirit win
For that's all done right here.
We can take to do this way or of God's Ways..

August 22, 2022
By SherAnne Shea Jubelirer

ON NOW A HOT SUMMER DAY

We do listen to Creedance Clearwater Revival.
That's some good music!
That's my father's song, Travelling Band.
Boy, do I ever love my Dad.
That's before whereas my mother was reminding me on
what to do somewhere.
For we do look together out @the unchanging sea.
By now, I do feel this need to find a new place to live.
Jeff, my great American Poet, holy husband was telling
me, its alright
For us to be here for that's right here,
And look a while, Sherry has to do that.
We do think hopefully, that Jesus has already given us
of that's eternal life
And of that's eternal love and of that's eternal wisdom.
So we do believe God's Mercy was even forever for us.
And we were believing that God was waiting for
us likewise.

July 3, 2022
By SherAnne Shea Jubelirer

ON THAT'S DREAMS

I only wish upon a setting sun
And I dreamed upon a shooting star out of the sky
Only then I opened the Holy Word Of God to the place
of that's wisdom
As I carefully thought to make a day of writings
By reason of the hope within
Only then, God in his graciousness was wonderfully
beautiful to me
And I had that's dreams of living the writer's life inside
my soul.
Quickly I took the promises for this was mine
And I kept my head and heart together
As I remembered dreams like this
And would never give up
So I do prayers for now
To live the life we have long dreamed of
As masterpieces are now being created by us
Of all days
That others are awaiting on
And by and by
On these good days of my life right here...

By SherAnne Shea Jubelirer

FOR ALL THAT WALKING THAT I WAS DOING AND TAKING FIXER WITH, US IN GOD ALMIGHTY

On that's walking on in God, getting
That's my walk on
And coming this way by prayers
And by thinking of my full life here.
And niceness is absolute code before me
And that's before my very face of doing readings
And doing writings and that's work on the computer
way up here.
And while I make prayers
And hope God does see all of us, Shea's.
And whenever I do talk to myself, sweetness
And kindness comes to myself
And I do pray that's on God's Will daily.
We were walking everywhere and wholesomely!

June 16, 2016
By SherAnne Shea Jubelirer

THAT'S OVER AND THAT'S OVER AS THAT'S MY PAST

I was pondering thought and I was thinking right
here...
I do have a place where we can think together
And only of memories and wishes and dreams and by
prayers, often
And by transpired actions done daily
As that's now influencing my present reality.
That's my past of fires was never changing except I do
think that's envitable...
I do have that's God's acceptance
And that's God's forgiveness
And I do think and I do believe that's a roaring fire but
they are just only my own memories of its mind,
Simply remembered days and words and ideas
And how alive in my own reflections,
We are of this present thought.

By SherAnne Shea Jubelirer

THAT'S TOGETHER AGAIN

And that's again I am reminiscing
And remembering and thinking with you at my side
right here.
Maybe the prayers we said
That were asked so often by heart were now coming to
be real true.
I do only wish we had trusted in divine providence more
readily
For I do think we would have been more understanding
with that.
Now no turning back must be
For only sunshine and truths of graces
I do now only see that!

By SherAnne Shea Jubelirer

WE MUST LOOK!

Look I am looking, I do need to take a stand for life
toward the people around us Shea Jubelirer's.
I have been very picky
And where we do live its feeling and sounding like we
are near a lot of people.
Simply no is the answer behind closed doors or Jesus is
the answer for
I only do face to face or over the phone.
I need to realize I am in control of my responses.
Likewise, we can do on a radio show again
Or maybe in the newspapers
Whenever we are good and whenever we are ready
Or already.
We are in communications and media
Writing and publishing.

By SherAnne Shea Jubelirer

WE MUST MAINTAIN!

And now to write these morning pages
And to say anything to do about God Almighty!
Likewise to maintain whatsoever or what to do
While I must wait on the Lord Jesus to give
me anything
That we may have need of.
For I was given I do like to do this
And I do like to do that
For I was that's real true to do good things of
God Almighty.
I will listen to Family Radio Station, 990am
And choose to be doing some more prayers.
We do realize prayers are needed.
I was told I am needed by Dr. Wilf
And Fr. Gus and my father agreed for that.
And supposedly we have been very important
According to my doctors and priests.
Authors are supposed to be very important
And where as attending church and maintaining health
is very important.
Jesus is my very health and wholeness and life.
Jeff and I like we need to do this together.
Except I do take this went to the catholic churches.
O Lord Jesus, be Thou of my visions and dreams
And Jesus, the Christ be Thou my wisdom!
For that's pretty powerful and that's pretty neat
To pray and to write and to think and to do prayers
again and again.

WE DO TAKE ROAD TRIPS

We took road trips, for years, we have already done so
and we had to do so.

And that's only my father's doing, he loves taking
the road.

They were in the town where Lisa and Jonathan and his
2 girls live recently.

Kelly was the driver and these 3, my mother and my
father took the road to Connecticut

For a few days.

Road trips are wanted and are ironically very memorable
like whenever Rick Shea and Steven Michael Shea
and me were driving from Minneapolis, Saint Paul to
Atlanta and back again to Minneapolis, Saint Paul.

The three of us were young enough and we were getting
high on marijuana and hanging out together, listening
to the radio and driving.

When we arrived in Nashville, Tennessee, they were
buying fireworks along side the road.

We loved one another and had a very good
time together.

Likewise, we took the highway from Philly to
Connecticut often. That's whenever my folks lived in
Monroe, Connecticut. Connecticut to Philadelphia.

Whenever I was in college, we took a road trip to Colorado and Wyoming and snow skied Jackson Hole, Wyoming. We all were on a bus together.

Us girls were talking and kissing a different guy every night while we were staying at Teton Village, Wyoming.

More road trips were done. That's a good idea to take a road trip!

EXPERIENCES AND LIFE
IN CONNECTICUT

We lived in Monroe, Connecticut for some years. A small, quiet town in Southern Connecticut.

For whenever that's my father's doing where he had been a very successful Chief Executive Officer for Pepperidge Farms in South Norwalk, Conn. When you purchase Pepperidge Farm Breads, my father said its supposed to be! And I do remember we took walks a lot and had to drive everywhere. In Monroe, my father's yard was called Shea Park. And while I was in Connecticut, John Potak and Frankie were my 2 boyfriends. John Potak took me to a very nice restaurant of a waterfall over a water damn and together, we were having drinks and dinner. We met at a prayer meeting at Saint Jude Holy Catholic Church in Monroe. But my folks didn't like him much so I left him.

Whenever I met Jeffrey David Jubelirer, he wrote him a letter and that was sent to him. John was furious since I was supposed to marry him. I had left him so that was that. Likewise, I was on dates with Frankie, a pretty, nice young black man. He was with me whenever I was weeping since I needed medicine for my psychosis back in those days.

One night, he took me to a black bar and I was the only one who was white at the bar. Everybody was so nice to me. We smoked, drunk beer and danced together.

Frankie used to say to me, where to? The bar or the church? We were very cute together.

John said Frankie was not exactly the caliber, John my boyfriend was, supposedly looking back here, they were both good boyfriends. That's so over with by now. Since I left out of Monroe, to finish that sure diploma at Rutger's University, over in Camden, New Jersey.

THAT'S PURPLE HEART PRAYERS

Sedated, underrated
And left to my own devices.
I do know I am alone in my thoughts
So I will pray for control
And make Jesus to be my sanity.

There are many players
But none wins.
All trip on love.

Constantly doing prayers
And hope for love grows stronger
On the light of that's purple heart prayers.
Truth is spoken here.
I am telling you now.

By SherAnne Shea Jubelirer

THANKS BE TO GOD

Thanks be to God! I am truly thinking of Jesus everyday! I truly do think of Jesus, the Christ everyday of my life up till now and I will be thinking of Jesus forever because I can side with Jesus. For all of my life, I thought of Jesus and was doing prayers especially since I was only in my 20's. I have become religious and spiritual since this time or since then only was Jesus. However, my dearest father

Would tell me then for he was so concerned for me. We were playing like I was another wife for him.

May God Almighty bless for they were always together. God bless his holy soul and spirit. May Jesus do for that holy couple forever. That would be psychiatrist lady is my name for that's only my mother. She truly does Jesus and thee Blessed Mother and Queen. They have been together, travelling all over this world and travelling together.

Now they take care of one another and set great examples of the good life and professionalism and they like to be do-gooders and do spiritual works of mercy for all of us in our family. And they have many friends.I do sow pieces of writings and sow wholesomeness for all of us. My brothers do love me. They love everyone. Whatsoever our love is very strong and only and is the foundation of all our big, very educated, hard working, catholic, christian family.My father has said God Almighty has been very good for him. I truly do by that. I do realize God has great kindness for us, maybe my family as very well likewise. For now, that's real true for me to be writing of this regarding my whole family. I truly do love everyone of us even if we were gone and far and wholesomely in other towns and places. That's over due to money now.Whatever my father has done or finished was anything was of his CEOHood and presidency. I was told I can do anything likewise. He is filled of great wisdom like my mother and prayers have been made at the prayerline, that we would be able to reap of that's great wisdom and keeping of that and learning of that without losing that.

We were reading that book, SIMPLE TRUTHS and great men with great wisdom are sometimes doubted or never given proper credit, that they truly earned. Mother Teresa is the Author of that book.

As I write this right here, I said good night!

ON THAT'S SLEEPING IN WOULDS FOR WORK AND THAT'S WORKING

Perhaps at daybreak, I will be a sound a sleep like a doe
in the forest where
Everything will be silent by me with
My holy husband right by my side.
Deep through the night,
We will dream
And think of that's only our brothers far gone in other
places of our country
And of that's again whenever we will laugh together
trying to be funny and sweet.
Our communication capabilities have expanded because
of high technology.
Life is pretty good
Whenever loved ones are in reach
And right now we are all healthy and strong.
That's gratefulness often thought of in prayers.
Quietly now I will gather my thoughts for prayers…

By SherAnne Shea Jubelirer

ON SOME THOUGHTS OF DAY

And now that's a goal learning with access to the Internet. And so many companies are available online.

And I am posting on Linkedin.com, FaceBook.com, UpTrends.com, Google, Instagram and on.

That's a wealth of information online and Angela, my holy girlfriend says we must protect that! And I am so lucky, that I met Salena Billings on Linkedin.com. Together we were doing a business selling Easy1Up

And digital software and we had done a zoom video and she bought one of my books. As with businesses online, its never successful for me since they require more money than I am willing to make an investment. I did back out of this business, Easy1Up except I was posting on UpTrend.com

During that's now past. I was with Shaklee briefly with Debra. I did back out of this business as well. Shaklee is an old business that I could return to suppose I was interested.

I do realize that takes months to begin making and earning all kinds of money. And I do realize I do need to do this right here. All that for now. Ok, things are often very good or that's fine for us now. I do take that's mine has, call us nevers!

By SherAnne Shea Jubelirer

ON RESTORE OF MY CREATIVE ENERGIES, MY MORNING PAGES

And where to begin a very good new day, I do write for my morning pages on the Artist's Way program In order to restore my creative energies. And this is a great, new day here! Except I do have over this insomnia, since some nights I do have trouble getting to sleep and some nights I do wake up too early. And yet I was given I do like to do this and I do like to do that. So I was doing prayers. Whenever I first awaken, I do believe God Almighty has all of us and that He has heard my prayers. I was listening to Family Radio Station and I was reading along in my bible as they were reading the book of Daniel. It was interesting. Particularly when the book was talking of visions Daniel had. And this is beginning of a new week in March. We are doing so much for appointments and work. And now I do realize my day will require that I do take a higher power nap. I maybe so tired, I will need some more sleep. And right now, I was blank before I am to finish these 3 pages. Except I can keep on writing practically anything to do that I can think of. For this radio station is wild. I said enough. That's enough said. I sure said this!

By SherAnne Shea Jubelirer

WITH LIFE, ITS ON FORTH WITH

A new beginning of nearness and future.
And of memories of how I may have been
more principled
And had that's powers of agreement more readily over
past days.
A difficult man is the poet except he just only told me
life gets easier
And he truly is a poor man in Philly.
Except I do love him deeply and greatly.
For indeed and before me to do good
And to do anything worthy for the Lord Jesus Christ
So I do write any books and any writings and come
to church;
As my good works.
I do wish all others well except God Almighty is truly
who I do seek.
God does love others and Jesus, the Truth will help us
endure trouble and love and life
In heaven and above.
Maybe great things take time for completions and doing
well to be given by God of infinite graces
And maybe this Author can build words and ideas
And make sure ideas and thoughts of God are made
And while of friends to be of approval

Whenever us good Catholics come together for prayers
and righteousness and holiness.
We must overcome all negativity
As hopefully Jesus saves us, all of us for we do good
works and let Jesus do all the good works And
I do begin again to set ourselves for prayers and
understanding and wisdom.
And this is done today last day of 2012.

THAT'S FOR MY WRITING LIFE

He gently kisses me
Then we do feel each other's passion for writings.
I was of that's a long time where I was beginning to
hope for more self control
And respect.
Ideally that's love and respect.
In the rush of that's moods that long for expression
And creativity,
I do think and dream about creating words and ideas
On its written pages and pages
Flying forth
And always these many words on paper and in that's our
books are
To be my delight.

For I am with the Poet and dreaming
While my writing life has my soul growing
And doing readings
And while wanting to chew
And digest the words
And read them to the Poet,
So much to do to my joy!

THAT'S TRUE LOVE TO STRENGTHEN

You strengthened me today with
Your compassionate words of assurance
That you told me
We would be able to make things work.
Sweetness of success
We would soon experience
As I became less worried
And you, my holy husband held me tenderly.

By SherAnne Shea Jubelirer

THAT'S THE HOLY SPIRIT IN US

For whosoever will walk in the Holy Spirit,
Salvation is promised to be won.
With faith to overcome and win
Determining and seeking to be of miracles in Jesus who
is glorified by God Almighty,
For He is the giver of all good and perfect gifts
That are by graces of faith that believes
While Jesus even does forever create us and He is doing
prayers for all of us
Within faithful prayers made often by us
And good actions are taken
Where growing knowledge and graces of the
Truth of Jesus and its mysteries and the Way of Jesus
and the Life given by Jesus,
We relax and rest and hope
And so we do keep on doing that which is more
wonderfully beautiful and good While we sure do seek
by faith that's love and that's hope daily.

By SherAnne Shea Jubelirer

THAT'S SPIRITUAL THINGS

I have realized I am about to find more graces in
our souls because I do know through daily prayerful
contemplations and smiles with kind gestures I may
acquire that's life eternal by thinking and doing right
kinds of things. For it is only then I can reach and dwell
upon unseen realms of truths. For I look inside my soul
of growing mystic faith by studying spiritual things
unseen. Now I will pray and sing and compare spiritual
things with the spiritual.

By SherAnne Shea Jubelirer

ON SEA DAYS

Only then I was walking an unending place upon
the empty beach
And pretended I was completely alone.
I was left for protection and within was my admiration
for that's only of my father's doing
And thoughts of contemplative stance made I of sea
waves that wisked and constantly was coming forth
Upon the unknown ways of my fate
Of hope forever given to the truth found inside together
of holy scriptures, I read upon the pages of Malachi.
For with rememberances of Jesus's name, are my
thoughts arisen by praises forever more
Of worship upon the majesty
I could then only see for I was above that vision in the
skies of an Atlantic tapestry.

By SherAnne Shea Jubelirer

THAT'S JOY

Happy to be at a very nice hotel out in Center City
As I relax in the lobby.
Suppose I had wanted a spicy virgin mary,
This was mine at my request.
For the moment I take pleasure
At watching the people.
While I am ever hopeful
For I do think of how I will work out for my life
Day by day
In prayers and meditations
On the Holy Scriptures
Ever hopeful I will become more mystical
By dreams
I do keep alive inside my heart now growing.

By SherAnne Shea Jubelirer

ON A NEW DAY, A SPIRITUAL AWAKENING

Putting God in all of my life, putting Jesus in all of
my life
And putting the Holy Spirit in all of my life.
And while I was at Holy Mass tonight
I was experiencing that anointing of the Holy Spirit,
While doing prayers, where I felt that.
And that anointing of the Holy Spirit is so real
And I am having to do of myself.
I am supposed to be holy.
God's Will be done!

By SherAnne Shea Jubelirer

TILL WE ARE WITH GOD ALMIGHTY

Such wonders upon dreams of our excellent and great writings and launching our very good writing careers in 2010. Us 2 poets and writers, Authors Only profoundly in love and living that's 2 of us for writing life

And that's holy life together with our little dog named Fixer. That's our dreams of seeing miraculous brilliant and very smart thoughts

Of things that we were thinking to be very well put together upon the written pages. Its pages and pages of writings that we sure do. And for holy dreams with hope arising. Truly for that now, truly only then.

We are seeing great things do happen in our connections and good works for this works and that works right here…Joy is evident. We will work on forever to grow these holy dreams and visions where that's true freedom and that's rights of privilege are actualized and the life of Jesus inside of our souls and spirits

Are truly maintained.

Till we become ashes and dust, till we are with God Almighty.

By SherAnne Shea Jubelirer